ry Makers

Anne Frank
...and her diary

Sarah Ridley

SEA-TO-SEA
Mankato Collingwood London

This edition first published in 2013 by
Sea-to-Sea Publications
Distributed by Black Rabbit Books
P.O. Box 3263, Mankato, Minnesota 56002

Printed in the United States of America,
North Mankato, MN

9 8 7 6 5 4 3 2

Published by arrangement with the Watts
Publishing Group Ltd, London.

Library of Congress Cataloging-in-Publication Data

Ridley, Sarah, 1963-
  Anne Frank-- and her diary / Sarah Ridley.
    p. cm. -- (History makers)
  Includes index.
  ISBN 978-1-59771-391-7 (library binding)
1. Frank, Anne, 1929-1945-- Juvenile literature. 2. Jewish
children in the Holocaust-- Netherlands-- Amsterdam--
Biography-- Juvenile literature. 3. Jews-- Netherlands--
Amsterdam-- Biography-- Juvenile literature. 4. Amsterdam
(Netherlands)-- Biography-- Juvenile literature. I. Title.
  DS135.N6F73545 2013
  940.53'18092-- dc23
  [B]
                          2011049890

Series Editor: Jeremy Smith
Art Director: Jonathan Hair
Design: Simon Morse
Cover Design: Jonathan Hair
Picture Research: Sarah Ridley

Picture credits: Anne Frank House/
Getty Images: 5, 6, 9, 13, 20, 22.
AKG Images: front cover left, 7.
Hulton Archive/Getty Images: 12, 17.
Longhurst/Topfoto: 15.
Picturepoint/Topham: 23.
Roger-Viollet/Getty Images: 21.
Michael Teller/AKG Images:19.
Three Lions/Hulton Archive/Getty Images:
18. Ullstein Bild/ AKG Images: front cover
right, 1, 10, 11, 14. George W Wales/Hulton
Archive/Getty Images: 8.

RD/6000006415/001
May 2012

Contents

The Frank Family

On June 12, 1929, Anne Frank was born in Germany.
Her parents already had a daughter named Margot.
The family was Jewish and had many friends, both Jews and Christians.

▶ Margot (left) and Anne (right) with their father, Otto Frank, in 1930.

June
1929 ▷

Anne Frank is born.

October
1929 ▷

Worldwide money crisis.

5

Early Life

As a small child, Anne played in the backyard and on the street.

Anne liked to play in the sandbox. Here her mother stands close by.

1930s ▶

Support for the Nazi Party grows.

January
1933 ▶

Hitler and the Nazi Party take power in Germany.

Adolf Hitler salutes some German soldiers.

Anne's parents began to worry about the new leader of Germany, Adolf Hitler. Hitler and the Nazi Party wanted to rid Germany of Jews and other people whom they did not see as German.

March
1933 ▶

The Nazi Party starts to send people to concentration camps.

April
1933 ▶

The Nazi Party begins to make laws against Jews.

7

The Franks in Amsterdam

Like many Jewish families, the Franks no longer felt safe in Germany. They moved to Amsterdam in the Netherlands in 1934.

These Jewish children were sent by their parents to safety in England.

1930s ▶

Thousands of Jews leave Germany.

1934 ▶

The Franks move to the Netherlands.

Anne and Margot soon felt at home in their new apartment. They made friends, went to school, played sports, and went on trips to the seaside.

Anne's father liked to take photographs. This one shows Anne (second from left) and her friends on her 10th birthday.

1938 ▶

The Germans take over Austria and parts of Czechoslovakia.

June
1939 ▶

Anne's 10th birthday.

World War II

The German army marched into the Netherlands in 1940.

In 1939, Germany invaded Poland. England and France declared war on Germany. Then the German army invaded the Netherlands.

1939 ▶	April 1940 ▶	June 1940 ▶
World War II begins.	The German army invades the Netherlands.	France surrenders.

▲ Anne studied hard at school.

At first, Anne's life stayed much the same. She went to school, did her homework, and played with her friends.

June
1940 ▷

Anne's 11th birthday.

December
1940 ▷

Otto Frank's business moves to 263 Prinsengracht, Amsterdam.

Jews under Attack

But life began to change. Jewish children had to go to Jewish schools. Jews were not allowed to travel by tram, bus, or car. Many lost their jobs.

All Jews over the age of six had to wear a yellow star with "Jew" written on it.

April
1941 ▶

The Germans give out identity cards to all Dutch people.

December
1941 ▶

The United States joins the war, fighting on Britain's side.

In June 1942, Anne's parents gave her a diary for her 13th birthday. She decided to write to the diary as if it were a friend named Kitty.

Anne's diary. She began each entry, "Dear Kitty."

1942 ▶

The Germans make laws about what Dutch Jews may or may not do.

June
1942 ▶

Anne's 13th birthday.

The Secret Annex

Anne's father prepared a hiding place for the family. He was afraid that the Germans would send them to concentration camps.

This photo shows Anne not long before she went into hiding.

June 29th
1942 ▶

The Germans state that all Dutch Jews will be sent to camps in Germany.

When Anne's sister, Margot, was ordered to enter a camp, the family had to act. They fled from their apartment and moved into the hiding place, called the Secret Annex.

◄ The Secret Annex was above and behind Otto Frank's office and storeroom. The building is now a museum.

July 6th
1942 ▶

The Frank family goes into hiding.

1942 ▶

Battles are fought around the world.

Life in the Secret Annex

Mr. and Mrs. van Pel's room

Peter van Pel's room

It was a shock for Anne to live in such a small space. Soon the van Pels family and a dentist, named Mr. Pfeffer, joined them.

Otto, Edith, and Margot Frank's room

Anne had to share a room with Mr. Pfeffer

This drawing shows the rooms in the Secret Annex.

July 13th
1942 ▶
The van Pels family enters the Secret Annex.

November
1942 ▶
Mr. Pfeffer arrives.

Many Jews went into hiding in the Netherlands, like these people who lived under the floorboards of a house.

Anne wrote in her diary saying how much she missed her friends, her freedom, and her cat. Still, she knew that she was lucky to be safe.

1942 ▶

Thousands of Jewish prisoners are dying in concentration camps.

The Helpers

Four workers at Otto's business agreed to bring food, books, and clothes to the Secret Annex. They risked their own lives by doing this.

During the war, people all across Europe often had to line up for food. These people are on a French street.

1942 ▶

Food shortages and food rationing.

1942 ▶

The war continues with battles on land, in the air, and at sea.

During office hours, the Frank family and their friends had to be very quiet in case anyone heard them. They could not run a faucet or flush the toilet.

The helpers built a bookcase in front of the stairs to the Secret Annex, to hide it from the other workers.

June
1943

Anne's 14th birthday.

July
1943

There is a burglary in the offices below the Secret Annex.

Anne's Secret Life

Anne recorded her friendship with Peter van Pels, shown here.

Anne wrote about everyday life in her diary. She kept busy by reading, doing schoolwork, learning new skills, and helping out. She hoped to be a writer after the war.

1943 ▶

The war is not going as well for Germany.

1944 ▶

Anne's friendship with Peter develops.

April
1944 ▶

Another burglary in the offices downstairs.

German soldiers gather up Polish Jews to send them to concentration camps.

In her diary, Anne described how scared she was of being discovered. Sadly, her fears came true.

June
1944 ▶

The British and other forces invade Normandy in France.

June
1944 ▶

Anne's 15th birthday.

Discovery!

On August 4, 1944, men stormed into the Secret Annex. They sent everyone to concentration camps. Anne Frank died in a concentration camp in 1945, like six million other Jews. Out of the people who had lived in the Secret Annex, only Anne's father, Otto Frank (right), survived.

August 4th
1944 ▶
Police enter the Secret Annex.

September 4th
1944 ▶
The inhabitants are sent to concentration camps.

October
1944 ▶
Margot and Anne enter the Bergen-Belsen camp

After the war, Otto discovered that one of the helpers had kept Anne's diary. He decided that other people should read Anne's words and the diary was published in 1947.

Anne's diary. Millions of people have read it worldwide.

February/March 1945 ▶	May 1945 ▶	1947
Margot and Anne die.	World War II ends in Europe.	*The Diary of Anne Frank* is published.

Glossary

Concentration camp A prison camp. The Germans sent Jews and others to concentration camps, where millions of people lived and died in horrible conditions.

Hitler Adolf Hitler was the leader of the Nazi Party in Germany.

Identity card A card that states a person's name, age, and maybe religion. The Germans used identity cards to find Jews more easily.

Invasion When one country sends its army into another country.

Jew Someone of the Jewish race or religion.

Laws Rules made by a government.

Nazi Party The National Socialist Party founded by Adolf Hitler.

Rationing Restricting the amount of food or goods to make sure there is enough for everybody.

Index